JOKES

The Tiny Book of Scottish Jokes

Des MacHale

Illustrated by
Graham Thompson

HarperCollins*Publishers*

HarperCollins*Publishers*
77–85 Fulham Palace Road,
Hammersmith, London W6 8JB

www.**fire**and**water**.com

This paperback edition 2000
1 3 5 7 9 8 6 4 2

Previously published in Great Britain
by Angus & Robertson (UK) 1988

ISBN 0 00 710494 4

Set in Stone Sans by Rowland Phototypesetting Ltd,
Bury St Edmunds, Suffolk
Printed in Great Britain by BemroseBooth Ltd

Jock (anxiously): 'You'll have to help me Doctor McTavish, I can't stop stealing things.'

Dr McTavish: 'Take two of these pills after meals.'

Jock: 'What happens if they don't work?'

Dr McTavish: 'Get me a crate of Scotch.'

Have you heard about the Scotsman who gave a waiter a tip?

The horse lost.

A little Scottish boy burst into the house and said to his father: 'Daddy, Daddy, I ran home behind the bus and saved ten pence.'

His father replied, 'You could have done better son. You could have run home behind a taxi and saved fifty.'

Scottish preacher to his congregation: 'I don't mind your putting buttons in the collection plate, but please provide your own buttons and don't pull them off the church cushions.'

Scotland is noted for its close family ties. Jock was one of nine children and when his wife died after forty years of marriage he never shed a tear. He explained to his friends – it wasn't as if she was a blood relation.

Jock was in London wearing his tartans when a curious lady asked him if there was anything worn under the kilt.

'No, madam,' he replied with a flourish. 'Everything is in perfect working order.'

There are many theories about the bagpipes, otherwise known as the missing link between music and noise.

Some say they were invented by a Scotsman who trod on his cat and liked the noise.

Others claim that they are based on the noise made by a dying octopus.

However, the truth is that they were given to the Scots by the Irish as a joke – but the Scots haven't seen the joke yet.

Another Scottish preacher is said to have prayed thus after a particularly unproductive collection: 'We thank you Lord that the plate was returned safely.'

McTavish was dying so he asked if a piper could be allowed into his hospital ward so he could hear the bagpipes for the last time.

McTavish recovered, but every other patient in the ward died.

How did the Grand Canyon come about?
A Scotsman lost a sixpence.

An American was hopelessly lost in the Highlands and wandered about for nearly a week. Finally, on the seventh day he met a kilted inhabitant.

'Thank Heavens I've met somebody,' he cried. 'I've been lost for the last week.'

'Is there a reward out for ye?' asked the Scotsman.

'No,' said the American.

'Then I'm afraid ye're still lost.'

McDougal, surprisingly, always travelled first class on the railways. It was the only way he could avoid meeting all his creditors.

Have you heard about the famous sign on a Scottish golf course?

MEMBERS WILL REFRAIN FROM PICKING UP LOST BALLS UNTIL THEY HAVE STOPPED ROLLING

A suitor was looking for Jock's daughter's hand in marriage. Jock asked him, 'Would you still marry my daughter if she had no money?'

'Yes I would, sir!' replied the poor lad eagerly.

'Then away with you,' said Jock. 'There are enough fools in the family already.'

Wedding guest: 'I believe that this is your third daughter to get married.'

McTavish: 'Yes, and the confetti is getting very dirty.'

A Scottish newspaper carried the following ad in its Lost and Found columns: 'Lost – a £5 note. Sentimental value.'

McNab was travelling by train seated next to a stern-faced clergyman. As McNab pulled out a bottle of whisky from his pocket the clergyman looked at him and said reprovingly, 'Look here, I am sixty-five years old and I have never tasted whisky in my life.'

'Don't worry,' smiled McNab as he poured himself a dram. 'You're not going to start now.'

How do you take a census in Scotland?
Throw a penny in the street.

Have you heard about the two Scottish burglars who were arrested after a smash and grab raid?

They were caught when they came back for the brick.

Englishman: 'In Scotland, the men eat oatmeal; here in England we feed it to our horses.'
Scotsman: 'That's why English horses and Scottish men are the finest in the world!'

Much may be made of a Scotsman, if he is caught young.

Samuel Johnson

Jock was at the zoo when he fell into a huge tank containing half a dozen man-eating sharks. However, he lived to tell the tale because he was wearing a T-shirt which said: SCOTLAND FOR THE WORLD CUP.

Not even the sharks would swallow that!

Why are Scotsmen so good at golf?

They realize that the fewer times they hit the ball the longer it will last.

It would require a surgical operation to get a joke into a Scottish understanding.

Rev. Sydney Smith

I hear McDougal left over a hundred thousand pounds when he died,' remarked McNab.

'McDougal didn't leave that money,' said McTavish, 'he was taken from it.'

Irate golfer, on his way to a round of 150: 'You must be the worst caddie in the world.'

Scottish caddie: 'That would be too much of a coincidence, sir.'

'Why, McTavish,' said the psychiatrist, 'you seem to have lost your stutter.'

'Yes,' said McTavish, 'I've been telephoning America a lot recently.'

Every week four Scotsmen got together to drink a bottle of whisky. One night, after many years of meeting, Jock said, 'I got some bad news today: I'm not long for this world, but when I pass on I'd like to think that when you meet you all keep me a dram and pour it over my grave.'

After a moment's silence one of the others asked, 'Would it not be better, Jock, if we gave it a swill round our kidneys first?'

The following was seen on a poster in Glasgow:
DRINK IS YOUR ENEMY.

Adjacent to this was another poster which said:
LOVE YOUR ENEMY.

I have been trying all my life to like Scotsmen and am obliged to desist from the experiment in despair.

Charles Lamb

A Scotsman had just put a pound on a horse and the horse came in at twenty to one. As the bookmaker handed him twenty-one pound coins the Scotsman examined each one of them carefully.

'What's the matter?' the bookmaker asked. 'Don't you trust me?'

'I'm just making sure that the bad one I gave you isn't among them,' said the Scotsman.

Sandy McTavish's nephew came to him with a problem.

'I have my choice of two women,' he told him, 'a beautiful penniless young girl whom I love dearly, and a rich old widow whom I can't stand.'

'Marry the girl you love,' said McTavish.

'I will follow your advice,' said the nephew.

'In that case,' said McTavish, 'could you give me the widow's address?'

Jock was playing golf with an elder of the kirk. On the last hole he missed a six-inch putt which cost him the match but, out of deference to his playing partner's status, he said absolutely nothing.

'That,' said the elder, 'was the most profane silence I have ever heard.'

The minister poured Jock a minuscule glass of whisky to celebrate the festive season.

'This whisky,' he told Jock, 'is nearly a hundred years old.'

'Is that a fact?' said Jock. 'Mind you, it's very small for its age!'

There are few more impressive sights in the world than a Scotsman on the make.

James Barrie

What's the difference between a Scotsman and a canoe?

A canoe sometimes tips.

They say it takes ten Welshmen to outsmart an Irishman, twenty Irishmen to outsmart an Englishman, and a hundred Englishmen to outsmart a Scotsman.

Jock was carrying his inebriated companion into a Temperance hotel.

'I'm sorry,' said the clerk, 'you can't bring him in here. This is a Temperance hotel.'

'Don't worry,' said Jock. 'He's far too drunk to notice.'

They finally picked up the Scottish obscene telephone caller.

He kept reversing the charges.

Have you heard about the Scotsman who never smoked cigarettes with his gloves on?

He hated the smell of burning leather.

A man called at Jock's door one evening collecting for the Home for Chronic Alcoholics.

Jock's wife answered the door. 'Call back after closing time,' she told the man, 'and you can have my husband.'

A little girl asked an elderly Scotsman for a contribution to a religious organization – 'money for the Lord' as she put it.

'How old are you, wee lassie?' he asked her.

'Ten years old,' she replied.

'Well, I'm eighty,' he said. 'I'm bound to see the Lord before you do and I'll give him the money myself.'

There was a terrible row at a Glasgow cinema the other evening. Two Scotsmen were trying to get in on the same ticket on the grounds that they were half-brothers.

McNab gave up reading the free newspapers at the public library because of the wear and tear on his glasses.

McDougal kept vigil at the bedside of his dying wife for several days. Finally he said, 'Agnes, I must go away on business now, but I'll hurry back. If you feel yourself slipping away while I'm gone, would you mind blowing out the candle?'

The Scotsman's dilemma: Whether to take longer steps to save shoe leather or shorter steps to avoid the strain on the stitches of his underpants.

Jock McTavish was due for a medical examination. As requested by the doctor, he took along a generous specimen in a large bottle. After the test the doctor said, 'You're fine. I couldn't find a thing wrong with you.'

Jock happily returned home and announced to his wife, 'Good news, Mary. You and I and the kids and Uncle Sandy are all in perfect shape.'

McTavish took his girlfriend out in a hired boat on the loch. It started to rain and finally it came down so hard that McTavish said, 'We're getting drenched. I wish the hour was up so we could row ashore.'

Jock was at a bitterly fought Rangers *v.* Celtic football match in Glasgow. The man next to him was terrified as the missiles flew over their heads.

'Don't worry,' Jock assured him, 'you won't get hit by a bottle unless it's got your name on it.'

'That's what I'm afraid of,' said the man, lowering his head further. 'My name is Johnny Walker.'

'What made you suspect that these two men were drunk, officer?' a Glasgow magistrate asked a policeman in court.

'Well, Your Honour,' said the policeman, 'Jock was throwing five pound notes away and Sandy kept picking them up and handing them back to him.'

McDougal heard about a doctor who charged ten pounds for the first consultation but only three pounds for every subsequent visit. So he waltzed into the doctor's surgery and announced, 'Here I am again, Doc.'

'Keep up the treatment I prescribed last time,' said the doctor, who was also a Scotsman.

'Daddy, who is that man running up and down the carriage with his mouth open?'

'Don't worry, son, that's a Scotsman getting a free smoke.'

Have you heard about the Scotsman who married a girl born on 29 February?

He had to buy her a birthday present only once every four years.

An Englishman, an Irishman and a Scotsman went into a pub. The Englishman stood a round, the Irishman stood a round and the Scotsman stood around.

A Scotsman took a girl for a taxi ride. She was so beautiful he could hardly keep his eyes on the meter.

The Scottish minister was preaching on the parable of the Good Samaritan. He felt he had better explain to his congregation why the priest had passed the victim by.

'And why do you think the priest passed him by?' he asked them rhetorically.

'Because he saw that the man had already been robbed,' came a voice from the back of the hall.

McDougal took his girlfriend out for an evening and they were back at the door of her flat just before midnight. As she kissed him goodnight she said, 'Be careful on your way home now, darling. I'd hate anyone to rob you of all the money you've saved this evening.'

They've stopped the crime wave in Scotland by putting a sign over the jailhouse saying:

ANYBODY CONVICTED AND PUT IN JAIL WILL HAVE TO PAY FOR HIS BOARD AND LODGING.

A Scotsman decided to give up pipe smoking for the following reasons:

1 When he used his own tobacco he never used enough to get a decent smoke.
2 When he smoked someone else's his pipe was always packed so tight he could never light it.

McNab has his doormat hung up in the hall to save the wear and tear.

McNab had counted his change four times at a shop counter.

'What's the matter?' asked the assistant. 'Haven't I given you enough change?'

'Yes,' said McNab, 'but only just.'

In Scotland they had to take pay-as-you-leave buses off the streets – they found two men had starved to death in one of them.

A lodger in a Scottish guest house was on his way to the bathroom when the landlady stopped him and said, 'Have you got a good memory for faces?'

'Yes,' he replied.

'That's just as well,' she said, 'because there's no mirror in the bathroom.'

Two robbers attacked a boarding house in Glasgow in search of money, and a fierce struggle resulted.

'We didn't do too badly,' said one as they counted the loot. 'We got twenty pounds between us.'

'But we had thirty before we went in,' wailed the other.

McNab was once run over by a brewery lorry.

It was the first time for years that the drinks had been on him.

You've heard of Irish coffee, but have you tried Scottish coffee?

It's hot water flavoured with burnt toast.

Have you heard about the Scotsman whose horse swallowed a ten pence piece?

He's been riding backwards ever since.

McDougal walked into a shop and asked for a cheap coat-hanger.

'Certainly sir,' said the shop assistant. 'Here's a nice one for five pence.'

'Don't you have anything cheaper?' asked McDougal.

'Yes, sir, a nail,' said the disgusted assistant.

'I was so sorry to hear that your wife died,' Sandy sympathized with Jock.

'You're not nearly as sorry as I am,' replied Jock. 'She had taken hardly any of those expensive pills I'd bought her.'

McDougal joined a hunting party in Canada.
After a time a large animal was sighted.

'What's that?' asked McDougal.

'That's a Canadian moose,' he was told.

'Well, I'd hate to see a Canadian rat,' he replied.

Jock's tooth was paining him so he decided to visit the dentist. As he sat nervously in the dentist's chair he fumbled in his pocket.

'There's no need to pay me in advance,' said the dentist.

'It's not that at all,' replied Jock. 'I'm just counting my money before you put me under gas.'

McTavish and McNab were out walking on a lonely road when suddenly they were held up by a mugger.

'Hand over all your money at once,' he ordered.

'Here's that fifty pounds I owe you,' said McTavish to McNab.

This fellow went to a Scottish doctor and said, 'Doc, I've got a very poor memory. What do you advise?'

'Well, you can pay me in advance for one thing.'

A Scotsman living in London was always boasting about his native land to his English friends.

'Why didn't you stay in Scotland,' one of them asked him, 'if it's such a wonderful place?'

'Well,' he explained, 'they were much too clever for me there, but I get on quite well here.'

Sandy and Jock dined together and after the meal Jock was heard to call for the bill for both of them. Next day the newspapers carried the headline: Ventriloquist found murdered.

How do you disperse an angry Scottish mob?
Take up a collection.

McTavish was travelling by rail in America. He asked the railway clerk for a ticket to Springfield.

'Which Springfield, mister?' asked the clerk. 'Missouri, Ohio, Illinois or Massachusetts?'

'Which is cheapest?' asked McTavish.

Stand behind your lover, woman,' shouted the Scotsman who had come home and surprised his wife with another man. 'I'm going to shoot you both.'

McTavish was taking his girlfriend for a drive on his motorbike. As they passed a hot dog stand she sighed, 'My, those hot dogs smell nice.'

'Hold on a moment,' said McTavish gallantly. 'I'll drive a little closer so you can get a better smell.'

It is now not generally believed that golf originated in Scotland.

No Scotsman would invent a game in which it was possible to lose a ball.

An elder of the kirk was surprised and disgusted to see Jock staggering out of his local boozer one night.

'Jock, Jock,' he chided him, 'and I always thought you were a teetotaller.'

'Yes I am, elder,' said Jock, 'but not a bigoted one.'

Have you heard the one about the Scotsman who gave an Englishman, a Welshman and an Irishman a present of twenty pounds each?

Neither has anyone else.

Just after McTavish had got married he said to the minister, 'I'm sorry I have no money to pay the fees due to you, but if you take me down to your cellar, I'll show you how to fix your gas meter so that it won't register.'

McNab will never forget the time he spilled a bottle of whisky on the floor by mistake.

He still has splinters in his mouth.

Jock had a pet dog so he decided to call it by a biblical name. He chose the name 'Moreover' because he remembered the biblical verse: 'Moreover, the dog came and licked his sores.'

Scottish football referees do pretty well financially. They get five pence back on every bottle.

A tramp decided he would shame McDougal into giving him some money, so he went on his hands and knees and began to eat the grass in McDougal's front garden.

McDougal stuck his head out the window and asked him what he was doing.

'I'm eating the grass,' said the tramp, 'because I'm starving.'

'Come on in,' said McDougal, 'and I'll let you into my back garden. The grass is much longer there.'

A minister during a church service noticed that the collection plate consisted of lots of pound coins and three pennies.

'I see we must have a Scotsman in the congregation,' he said jokingly at the beginning of his sermon.

A Scotsman at the back of the church stood up, and said, 'Your Reverence, there are three of us.'

It had been a bitterly cold day on the Scottish golf course and the caddie was expecting a handsome tip from his rich Scottish client.

As they approached the clubhouse the caddie heard the magic words, 'This is for a hot glass of whisky.' So he held out his hand and received a lump of sugar.

The Scots have an infallible cure for seasickness. You lean over the side of the ship with a ten pence piece in your mouth.

An old Scotsman was watching a game of golf for the first time.

'What do you think of it?' asked a friend.

'It looks to me,' was the reply, 'like a harmless little ball chased by men too old to chase anything else.'

McDougal received £10,000 for injuries received in a traffic accident while his wife received £2000.

'How badly injured was your wife?' a friend asked.

'Oh, my wife wasn't injured in the accident at all,' replied McDougal, 'but I had the presence of mind to kick her in the teeth before the police arrived.'

A Scottish proverb: Never drink whisky with water and never drink water without whisky.

W hat's the difference between a tightrope and a Scotsman?

A tightrope sometimes gives.

In a fit of Christmas spirit Sandy sent Jock a Christmas present – a homing pigeon.

Jock used to give his chickens the finest whisky to drink.

He thought they might lay Scotch eggs.

A Scotsman will never be insulted if you offer him a small glass of whisky – he will merely swallow the insult.

At an auction in Glasgow a wealthy American lost a wallet containing over £10,000. He made an announcement about his loss and added that he would give £100 to the finder.

From the back a clearly Scottish accent shouted, 'I'll give a hundred and fifty.'

Have you heard about the lecherous McTavish who lured a maiden up to his attic to see his etchings?

He sold her four of them.

'I hear Maggie and yourself have settled your difficulties and decided to get married after all,' Jock said to Sandy.

'That's right,' said Sandy, 'Maggie had put on so much weight that we couldn't get the engagement ring off her finger.'

A Scotsman had been presented with a bottle of fine old Scotch whisky which he placed in his overcoat pocket. On his way home he stumbled and fell and as he got up he felt a wet patch on his trousers.

'Please, Lord,' he prayed, 'let that be blood.'

Two Scotsmen had just arrived by rail in London from Aberdeen.

'That was a long and exhausting journey,' said one.

'And so it ought to be,' replied the second, 'for all the money it cost us.'

McDougal was sentenced to death by hanging. On hearing that it would cost £200 to have him executed in this manner, he said to the authorities, 'Look, give me twenty-five pounds and I'll shoot myself.'

Have you heard about the Scotsman who was suffering from alcoholic constipation?

He couldn't pass a pub.

A Scotsman and therefore an expert dram drinker was asked what he thought of Irish whiskey.

'It's useful stuff,' he replied, 'if you run short of water for diluting a Scotch whisky.'

A teacher asked Wee Jock, 'If you had a pound in your right-hand trouser pocket, and three pounds in your left-hand trouser pocket, what would you have?'

Wee Jock replied, 'Somebody else's trousers!'

McTavish, a millionaire of ninety-three, decided to marry a lovely young girl of eighteen. The preacher however, did not approve.

'I don't believe in marrying for money,' he told the couple.

'Good,' said McTavish. 'In that case I'll not offer you a fee for performing the ceremony.'

McTavish's little boy was being questioned by the teacher during an arithmetic lesson.

'If you had five pounds,' said the teacher,' and I asked you for three, how many would you have then?'

'Five,' said young McTavish.

The nervous candidate was being interviewed by the elders of the kirk to see if he was suitable to become their new minister.

'Are you a paper preacher?' they asked him.

'What on earth is a paper preacher?' he asked in dismay.

'If you write your sermons down on paper,' said one of the elders, 'then we know you will finish when there's no more paper. But if you don't, God only knows when you will finish.'

Two Scotsmen bought a bottle of whisky for a pound and it was the vilest brew they had ever tasted.

'I'll be very glad,' said one to the other, 'when we've finished this bottle.'

There was a Scottish baker who tried to economize by making a bigger hole in his doughnuts. He discovered that the bigger the hole he made, the more dough it took to go round it.

Jock used to say that he was a grand judge of a glass of whisky – and a merciless executioner.